RELUCTANT OPTIMIST

By Lauren Spooner

CONTENTS

II | OPTIMIST

PESSIMIST

PESSIMIST

I keep myself awake
Hoping tomorrow stays away
Just a little longer
Because I just got used to today
Sometimes my own skin feels
Like it's hanging on the wrong bones
Like it doesn't belong to me
And I can't seem to tell myself
Everything will be ok
Like I have a thousand times before
And all I feel is out of place
Like I was meant for something
Just out of reach.

TIRED

I want to be more than what I am
More than failures and lost chances
I Want to drive my own destiny
Whether or not I believe in it
I want to believe that I have a purpose
But it's hard most days
When things most people do easily
Are mountains nearly too difficult
For me to climb.
I'm exhausted with wanting
Wanting to be more
Wanting to be better
Wanting to feel more
Always wanting, never getting
I've learned to accept the way things are
I've learned that no matter how far I reach
I will always find a ceiling to hit
I will always fall back down
I do always get back up
But it's getting harder
To pick myself up off the ground
The dust I used to brush off
Is turning to mud that stains.
My knees are failing;
I am so tired,
I am so weak;
I struggle
Over and over again
But I don't know if next time
I'll want to find my footing again.

STILL

If I lie still enough
Sometimes my fear can't find me
Like a predator attracted to movement
It circles me, teeth bared
I keep escaping
With only scars to prove it was real
We're told over and over
The monster in the dark doesn't exist
And that may be true
Because this monster hunts in broad daylight
When I should feel the most safe
If I run, find a dark place and hide
Sometimes it can't find me
But sometimes it beats down the door
Turns on the light
And swallows me whole.

OF BIRDS & CAGES

There is a nest of birds inside my body
Trying to find their way out.
I can feel their wings beating
Bruises onto my insides

Their ever flapping wings
Stir my stomach into knots
That I can't hope to untie.

Every time I try to speak
My mouth fills with feathers
And I have to swallow hard
Again and again
To keep from choking on them.

They've pecked holes in my mind
These restless creatures inside me
So that I can't understand anything
The way I used to.

I know they are trying to escape
That they are trapped inside me
They mean me no harm, really,
Still, most days I feel
More like the caged bird
Than the cage itself.

ANXIOUS

You are a messenger in a bulletproof vest
Holding your palms out in surrender

You are flinch, twitch, and jump
At voices you can't stand to hear

You are nails chewed bloody
Nervous habits and red face

You are grit your teeth and bear it
When all you want is to be alone.

You are clawing fear under skin
And trying not to show it.

FOREST FIRE

Your forests are burning
And here I am
With a handful of matches
I did not light
Smoke stinging my lungs
While the flames lick
Afterimage patterns
Into the backs of my eyes
I never wanted you to burn
But sometimes all it takes
Is a spark
To destroy something.
These matches are not mine.
I did not light them;
I can't say the same
For the fire.

NOSTALGIA

We scraped our fingers over
The ashes of our youth
Trying to gather all the
Pieces we left behind
Running toward the future
Carefully going crazy
Over every word
We've ever said
Futilely grasping at
Every memory stripped away
Nostalgia is just a word
For memories
We have yet to tarnish
And people we
Didn't know we could lose.

NOTES

1.

I never did understand
The race to the finish
After all
We're all so small
in the end.

2.

The way to
My Heart
Is through my head
Since my brain
Thinks it's in control.

4.

Like an
Unfinished
Sentence
We are
All...

BIRD BONES

I am a bird,
Built from the bones of a girl

Muscle, skin, sinew
Twisted into a form with wings
A form that flutters and pecks
But cannot fly.

I am a bird,
flightless

Too heavy for the sky
And believe me when I say
Fying is harder
When your feet
Have never learned
To leave the ground.

I am a girl,
Built from the bones of a bird

Too fragile to fly
Too afraid of the open sky
Too afraid of feeling free
To realize I still have wings
Somewhere inside.

LESS THAN WHOLE

You learn to love the void inside you
Like was always supposed to be there
Like it was made just for you
Fits perfectly in your chest, in your head
Covers up the things that used to fit there
The things you used to remember loving
Don't have the same pull
As the black hole that is inside you now
You no longer know what it's like
To not feel like something is missing
Being less than whole feels
Like the only thing You were
Ever supposed to Be good at.

ESOTERIC

I wish I could draw circles
Signs and symbols
And have you understand
That there should be
More to life than this

The mundane
The days found lacking
The words that mean nothing
There is more than this
There has to be.

I cradle my head in my hands
And wish on a higher power
I draw sigils on my skin
And hope they mean something
Hope they make me more
Than what I am.

They don't,
They are nothing but inkblots
Open to interpretation
But nothing else
They are not important
I am not important

I cannot draw a line on the ground
And turn it into a wall
I cannot paint birds
And make them fly

I cannot stand in a circle
And be protected
I cannot call upon power
That I do not have.

I am not chosen or called upon
I just live in the world
I haven't changed it
The marks I make are superficial
They can all be erased.

TIME

I keep wondering if this is the end
Thinking about the days that didn't stretch on
The time I could have had

I live one second at a time
Not living for now
But stuck in moments that won't pass

I let the clock tick
Even if it's only counting down
The seconds I won't have.

There's no stopping it anyway.

THE END

It's all we can do to keep from being perfect
We are outlined in a sun that is always setting
Breathe in the exceptional stillness of this day
Exhale into a void so vast it steals our breath

We are becoming, always becoming
Never finished, never really ending
Ends become beginnings over and over
As we become part of the whole again

We keep our eyes on the sky
That won't keep it from falling
But we'll see the end coming
Much more clearly this way.

HEAD-ON

It's like this:
I have never been able to
Tackle my problems head on;
Seek them out and fix them.
I think and think and overthink
Until they're too far along.
Until my molehills are mountains
That I can't tunnel through anymore.

Later. That's my mantra.
I'll think about this later
I'll do that later.
I'll fix myself later.
Then later comes
And I can't look my past self
In the eyes and be honest
Can't just say
 "I'm sorry for doing this to you;
Let me help you now."

BLEEDING HEART

I am a bleeding heart
That no longer bleeds.
I have nothing left to give
But I still beat fruitlessly
Against a chest that feels
More like a cage,
Than a shield to protect me.
I am dried up and hollow
Unable to sustain even myself
But you keep squeezing,
Trying to draw out
One.
More.
Drop.

MONSTER

I have this thing
Curled up in my chest
Making a mess of my insides
Strangling my heart and lungs
Bending my spine
At all the wrong angles;
I don't know how to
Make it go away.
I've learned to swallow
Around my closing throat
To breath with lungs
That no longer want air.
I've learned that there is
A monster living inside me
But it doesn't want to escape,
It's already found it's home
Burrowed deep into my body
And it's
Not
Going
Anywhere.
I've gotten used to
Living with it
But that doesn't mean
It's not killing me.

SPASM

There is a twitch to me
Buried under my skin
There are moments
I am still
But underneath
I sit minutely shaking
And I could not
Tell you why
It happens
Only that it has
As long as I can
Remember.

Sometimes it's a spasm
A contraction of
Too many muscles
To ignore
Too many to stay still
Like a cold breath
On the back of my neck
There is no subtlety in this
I feel I am shaking off...
Something
I've never quite been sure
What exactly it is.
The saying goes:
"Someone is walking
Over your grave"
For every unexplained shiver
And sometimes I wonder
If somewhere there's a sidewalk
Built over my grave.

NEON WORLD

I am awash in the glow
Of a moon that
No longer exists
I turn up my face to howl
And find I've forgotten how.
The loss seems trivial
To a neon world.
The electric glow
That has replaced
That moon I knew so well
Wild things do not fit here
Even the birds scavenge
For man-made scraps
And shiny things
To add to their nest.

DESTINATION UNKNOWN

I guess it just feels strange
When everything around me changes
And I am stuck spinning my wheels
Wondering how to get moving again;
Feeling like I'm always halfway to somewhere
But never quite reaching a destination.
And I do love road trips
But sometimes you just want
To finally go home,
To sleep in your own bed,
To breathe familiar air.
Getting lost is only fun
When you are okay with it.
This constant searching for a place
That may not exist
Is exhausting
And I can't do it
Anymore.

RISE AND FALL

We rise like steam
Evaporating
As we reach out for the sky
Palms out, waiting
For something
We really want to hold on to

We fall like sunbeams
Warm
Waiting for someone
To sit with us
Hoping they don't
Stay long enough
To burn.

LIAR LIAR

My Anxiety is a liar.
It leans in at the worst times
Tells me things that I know
Are not true;
Tells me what it thinks I am worth
And it is never enough.

My Anxiety is a storm.
It blows apart
My playing card tower
Of self-worth over and over
Leaving me gathering the cards
And carefully rebuilding
Until it blows them down again

My anxiety is a monster
It rips my insides to shreds
Claws at my throat
Sits itself on my chest
So I can't breathe,
So I can't speak,
So I can't do anything
But watch it tear me apart
Piece by bloody piece.

TRUER WORDS

Rip the words from my throat
So I can't swallow them again.
The truth sits
Heavy in my chest
Waiting for someone to
Reach in and take it;
Bring it out into the light
For all the world to see.
And I stand here
Holding my bleeding throat
Coughing and choking
Pressing it back down again
Hoping no one will notice me
Trying to keep my heart
Where it belongs.

DARK SPACES

These blank spaces swallow you
From the inside out;
Extinguished lights leaving nothing
But shadows and smoke behind.

There are things in the shadows,
Creatures with sharper teeth than yours
And claws to rip your empty body open.
You can feel them crawling
Up your throat trying to escape

There is no moon tonight
No excuse for the wild thrum of madness
Winding it's way through your veins;
Except that it's always been there,
Hiding, just beneath the surface.

TIME LIMIT

There are seconds
Tick, tick, ticking
Beneath the curve of your smile
I wonder how long it will stay this time.

OPTIMIST

LIMINAL SPACES

3am parking lots,
Street light lit.
Empty offices,
Early morning fluorescents.
Airports with no crowds.
There is meaning there.
If you are quiet enough,
Listen closely enough,
There is something more
In ordinary spaces
Turned strange with emptiness.
Delicate moments, places
Shifting between spaces
They exist and do not
Cannot be sought out
But can be found
When you are not looking.

SUPERNOVA DREAMS

We dream in supernovas
Synapses firing like newborn stars;
But in the end we
Find our way slowly,
Step by step.
We build new paths
Stone by stone,
Making sure
We are on solid ground
Ready for whatever
Comes next.

HEALING CRYSTALS

I keep stones around my neck
In drawers and boxes
To remind me
That there was a time
I believed in magic.
The rational mind
Is a funny thing
Because I wish
I could hold onto
That belief
Let it fill me and soothe me;
But I know the only magic
Held in crystals
Is the millions of years
Spent underground
Growing into something
People want to believe in
And maybe that's enough.

LUCKY CHARM

I sometimes see 11:11 on clocks
I heard once that this is good luck
But I'm having a having a hard time feeling lucky
Lately I'm stuck in an endless cycle
Of high hopes and disappointments.
I try so hard to find luck;
Throw salt over my shoulder,
Never walk under ladders,
Step over every sidewalk crack,
Cross my fingers and wish on stars
But it ends up meaningless.
I wish I could have faith in symbols.
I wish I could believe in lucky charms;
But I remain firmly grounded in reality
Looking up to the stars
Hoping for just enough magic
To make my luck real.

TRAVELLERS

We move along
Becoming highways
Side streets and backroads;
We flow like traffic
Standing still
Or moving too fast;
Dreaming of being
Somewhere
Other than where we are;
Ending up
For better or worse
Where we never expected.

SURVIVORS

We wore the night sky
Like bruises on our knuckles
From hitting too many walls
Made of stars and hope.

We are survivors now
Bruised but still standing;
Fighting back at the darkness
That drapes itself over our shoulders.

We wear our bruises like badges;
Showing off our battles
Both won and lost
Because we were survivors first.

We are warmed now
By the solidarity of matching bruises
By knowing we landed our punches
Didn't hold anything back

Survived.

REMEMBER

We remember things differently;
Different times, different places.
Songs from childhood,
Our favourite books.
Different yet the same;
Just far enough apart
To make us curious.
We can never experience
All of the same things
At the same time
And that's okay.
I want to hear
How you felt when you
Explored your own backyard
And I'll tell you about
The Creek behind mine
How cold the water was
How once I thought
I could run away
Into the mountains
And be free;
Blissfully unaware
Of the realities of nature,
Of the world.
I can't go back
But it's nice
To remember again.

MONUMENTAL

We stand at the feet of monuments
Questioning every truth we know,
Wondering what meaning we can find
In long standing stone and iron
Crumbling but still here.
Larger than any life
Before or after them.
We stand awed,
We tilt our heads back
Try to take in the magnitude
Of the far reaching past.
Then we turn
Walk away
Forget, eventually.
Go back to lives that seem
A little more mundane
Than they did before;
Try to get out from under
The shadows of the past
Without losing the wonder
That we found
When we were in them.

DREAMING

We are always seeking,
Finding ways to be new,
Finding ways to be okay again;
Dreaming of lives that are not ours.

We lie down at night
Closing our eyes,
Letting ourselves be still,
Letting ourselves dream again.

We live our lives in a daze
Imagining ways to be better
Imagining the things we would do
If only.
If only.
If only.

HANDHOLD

Do your eyes blur at the thought of falling down?
Well I can't count on my fingers and toes
The number of times falling down meant nothing but
Brushing the dirt off my clothes, mending the holes
Getting back up, and pretending I never fell at all;
And yes, sometimes I wish I would never get up again
And yes, sometimes the step I'm climbing is too high.
But sometimes there's a handhold, a rope,
Someone reaching down to help you back up,
And those are the times to be thankful,
Even if you never wanted or asked for help in the first place.
Being stubborn won't always get you to where you want to be
Sometimes, you have to stop saying no and say thank you instead,
And accept that not everyone thinks you owe them something.
Remember there are hands that will give to you
As much as there are hands that will take from you
Sometimes they're harder to see, keep looking.
Sometimes your hands need to give more than they take
Even when you think you have no more to give.
Try not to be blind to those who want to climb beside you
Don't ignore a handhold just because you didn't
Put it there yourself, no one will think less of you.
It's okay to be wary
Because no one wants more scars than they need,
And remember everyone's got a different way of coping
With the wounds they never saw coming.

FLIGHT

When I was small I used to wish
I could get lost in the spaces between walls.

That I could hide away in my own world
Like the sparrows that nested in our roof.

I thought about flying, spent most days
Looking at the sky and wondering what was out there.

I'd close my eyes and imagine I was a bird
Think about stepping off the roof of my house

Being unafraid of the open air, of the fall
Just to find out I had known how to fly all along.

GHOST STORY

I want to find the words
That mean I am still alive.
I am here, I am still breathing
I want to write this story
Without a cliff-hanger.
I want to settle into the words
To feel them rush through me;
Create strength in the
Curve of each letter.
I do not want to write a ghost story.
I do not want to be afraid
Of the spirits that live inside me
Haunting my bones,
Making the walls bleed and shake.
I don't think I can exorcise
The ghosts that linger here
But I want to tell them it's ok,
Your time here is over,
You can go now.
You can go now.
You can go now.

AMBITION

Wasted my youth
Somewhere between worry and apathy.
Telling myself not to hope too high
Things work out how they will.
Ambition is a dangerous creature
To be feared
But I was always edging closer
With a hopeful hand out;
Thinking maybe
I could touch it,
Just once,
Without worrying about
Being eaten alive.

REBUILD

Maybe bruises are like temporary roadmaps
To all of the places we've been;
They are ghost towns that disappear into time.
We know they were there,
We've seen them with our own eyes
But sometimes you can't rely on memory
And you have to dig up the foundations,
Prove that they were there
And rebuild.

NEW HOME

I am building a new home,
I *have* built a new home,
Away from expectation,
Away from you.
Can you blame me?
Of course you can, you do.
You always have.
You always will.
I am done shrinking
And I am not sorry
That I have built my home
Without a place
For you.

TIME BEFORE

The earth you stand on is
Older than you can fathom.
Millions of years
Of Ash, bone and rebirth,
Layer upon layer of ages gone by
Time you will never experience firsthand.

You hold uncountable eons
In your cupped palms as you
Fill them with earth;
You cannot know
How many lives were lived
In that palmful of dark soil.

Your toes time travel
As they sink into the earth,
You bring back eons under your fingernails
As you dig further back;
Trying to feel what the world was like
When it was still new
And time had yet to exist.

WE SLEPT HERE

We slept here
On the ashes and bones
Of a past not yet forgotten.
We dug our hands into the mess of it
Smeared our faces with the grime;
Like we could camouflage ourselves
Cover ourselves in the past
And never leave.

We slept there
For longer than we should have,
Unwilling to let go
Move on to more fitting beds,
To stop painting ourselves
In the colourless debris.
Hoping we could fade back into it.
Hoping we could revive it.
Hoping we could unburn our bridges.

We woke there
Forgetting too slowly
But finally forgetting
What it feels like to be grey;
Realizing that bones
Make for uncomfortable pillows
And that we'll never make
Warm blankets out of cold ashes.

REMINDERS

1.

    Sometimes the weight of
Your own mistakes will be too much,
You'll bend further than
You thought you could
And sometimes
You will break,

2.

    Sometimes it's the sting
Of someone else's mistakes
That hits you like a punch to the gut
And you'll sit
Trying to soothe your wounds
Wondering what you did wrong.

3.

    No one ever tells you
There will be times
You feel guilty for being happy,
Don't.

SHEEP'S CLOTHING

I am not a wolf in sheep's clothing,
Just a sheep with bloody hands
Who figured out
How to kill the wolf
But could never quite
Stomach becoming
The beast itself.

THIS TOO IS MAGIC

You can catch dancing particles of dust
In your hand, and call them magic
Because they disappear when you open it again;
And maybe there is a little magic there
Hidden in the fibers of my carpet
But dust settles and is swept away,
It cannot dance forever.
The sun won't stream soft and warm
Through my bedroom window every morning
But I'm okay with slate grey skies
With the ticking of rain on my window
This too is important, somehow.

STATIC OBJECTS

We speak as one stone to another
In silent millennia
The slow language of erosion
And the decay of time around us

We are static objects
The universe spinning around us
While we stare at star trails
And wish we could be meteorites

Maybe we were falling stars once
Flaring and fading too quickly
Maybe we were once young and on fire
Maybe being still really is our reward.

SURVIVAL

This is not the first time nor the last
That fear spins inside of you
Making carnival rides of your insides.
It is not the first time, no
But it always feels that way.
As the bottom drops out
Down is the only way to go
And your heart sticks in the back of your throat
Like the last time, and the time before,
But you can't remember surviving those falls either
Not really, you only know that the ground has shifted
And you are suspended in the air, waiting to drop
Struggling to get air into your faltering lungs
And never remembering that last time,
You survived.

BETTER

The thing is
Usually
Wanting to be better
And actually
Being better
Are concepts
Too different
To coexist

Sometimes change
Takes so long
To happen
You think it never will
Until it does
And most times,
It won't happen
Until you make it.

YOUNG AGAIN

Someday we'll be young again;
Not quite innocent
But naïve enough to be happy.
With enough time to sit still
And think about
How small we are
Compared to the stars;
And how we too could
Light up the sky
If only we weren't
Afraid To burn

SOMEWHERE

Somewhere out there
Is a sky so big
That you can't help
But feel small under it;
You'll stretch your hands
As wide as they can go
But still won't grasp
Any part of it
Big enough to
Make a difference.

Somewhere there are trees
Endless miles of dark forest,
Of sun dappled moss,
Of wild streams, murky ponds
Too dark or too cold
For you to want to swim in.
You'll leave them to their
Coldness, their darkness
And move onwards.

Somewhere out there
Is land so flat
You could walk across it
With your eyes closed
And reach the other side
Unscathed, but somewhere other
Than where you intended to be.
You will travel across this
Endless flatness
Feeling mountains in your veins
That you wish you could place here
But you never learned
How to build mountains
Only how to climb them.

NOT AFRAID

My dear, my dear, my dear
Say you are not afraid;
Say it so loud
That the doves in your body
Stop fluttering their wings,
So that you feel still for one moment.
Sigh like a pack of wolves;
Dangerous in the right situations
But mostly more afraid of you
Than you are of them.
You worry that everyone
Reads what you are thinking
By the way your
Face colours itself like a sunset,
By the way the light fades
Out of you, slowly.
Close your eyes,
Steady the thrumming
In your chest
You are not afraid
You are not afraid
You are not afraid
Anymore.

BRIGHT

Keep your
Head down,
Hands clean,
Soul quiet,
Leave your spirit
At the door
We are just
Trying to get by here.

But that's not it is it?
Let us see your shine
Be messy but
Keep your hands clean
When they need to be.
Let your soul speak loudly;
Let it lift those who hear
Even when you aren't sure
You like what it has to say
Trust, always
That it knows what to do.

HOPE

Hope is a delicate fluttering thing
Hold on too tight and it will die,
Swallow it and it will
Settle in your stomach
And live there for awhile
Lighting up your insides
Fluttering at the right times
Just enough so you know it's there;
But it is so easy to destroy,
So easy to forget about.
Sometimes it's too much to bear
And it has sharp edges
That cut when you least expect
That will sever it from you
When you need it most.

STRONG

My bones are heavy
Like I've been cast in cement
And I am strong, sure.
But this weight
Is more than I was built for.

They say lifting things
Means you get used to them,
Means they get easier to carry,
But the weight never eases
And I'm struggling under my strength.

I roll my shoulders
Soldier on
When all I want
Is to chip the cement away
Find out what I am
When I am not weighed down.

CANDLES

Light a candle
For every memory
You can't let go of.

Snuff one out
For every faded scar
That you won't let heal.

Burn circles
Into the palms of your hands
To remind you this is real.

You are still here
You are still here
Even if you don't know
What that means anymore.

HOME

I don't know if I believe that
We are all made of stardust or
Swirling galaxies of energy.
I know that my skin isn't
As thick as I'd like it to be
And the freckles on my body
Don't make constellations
Unless you know how to
Connect the dots.
I know that mountains and snow
Will always feel like home
No matter where I am;
And I know that home
Isn't always in the same
Place twice.
Sometimes you feel home
In waves, that make your heart
Feel lighter and heavier;
At the same time
Sometimes it's a moment in time
That you could spend your life
Trying to define.
Home is a dream, a photograph,
A stretch of highway,
An acre of forest that you've
Never thought to explore.
It's somewhere you know well
And sometimes somewhere
You've never been before.

BONES

Things end badly, like reversed implosions
I am spiralling outward, inward, in all directions.
I am shaking through my skin
Breathing ash and bone dust
As my flesh crawls with the need to burn
To strip itself away from the rest of me.
Sometimes I feel like it might be better
To exist as the bare bones of myself,
Stark white and exposed to the world
But still stronger than the paper skin
That covered me head to toe.

These bones are my foundation
The thing I've built my body around;
Scaffolding holding me up
Even when I don't want them to.
Sometimes I wish they'd break.
Sometimes all I want is to crumble
To sink to the floor
In an ungraceful slump of flesh and blood;
But these bones are strong,
Stronger than I deserve;
But they are here.
They are mine.
Even when I wish they weren't.

LIGHTER AGAIN

I live in this electric moment of sanity
I see everything as it is,
The reality of things
With the beautiful haze stripped away
And when I blink, it is still there.

I don't know if the air I'm breathing
Is the same air that surrounded me
A moment ago, but it feels different
I feel heavier, like every step
Makes footprints in concrete.

If I close my eyes for long enough
Sometimes it will go away
This clarity, this unrelenting realism
Maybe I'll feel lighter again
If I close my eyes tight and think of flying.

LOW TIDE

Hey don't forget to dream
When the lights go out.
Don't let the turning of the world
Make you restless.
Don't let every wrong footstep
Leave its mark in your mind.
You can't erase the past
But you can hope for a future
That doesn't leave you
Dreamless, Drifting, and lost
In a tide of missed opportunities.
You are salt water
And the golden reflection
Of the sun on the sea.
Pay attention to the sound
Of the water rising in your bones
As your breath rushes out
Like low tide
Leaving only those things
You no longer need.

OPTIMIST

I am an optimist
Despite all that has tried to take that from me.
There is a steady thrum of "Everything will be okay in the end"
That runs itself through my veins,
Even when things are at their worst.
This isn't to say I never feel hopeless
But I can't stay that way.
No matter how much I think I want
The sadness to stay,
It chips away like cheap paint
And I find out once again
That things really can work out for the better,
That there is more beauty in this world
Than we could ever know.
I want to live with the expectation
That beauty lies just around the next corner
Even if the journey to find it is long
It will be there,
Waiting.

ABOUT THE AUTHOR

Lauren Spooner grew up in Northwestern BC, Canada, and later moved to Greater Vancouver where she currently lives with her husband. Lauren has always been fascinated by words and their power and how she can mold them into something that speaks to a wide variety of people. Through her art and writing she explores the world, nature the human experience and her own emotions. She has previously written and designed "solipsism" a short zine of her poetry as well as "What doesn't Kill us..." a book of poetry and art created for her final project at the Art Institute of Vancouver. "Reluctant Optimist" is her first foray into self-publishing. When not writing, she works as a full-time in-house graphic designer, takes on freelance design work as well as creates and sells her own personal art in her free time.

You can find more about Lauren on Instagram
@LaurenSpoonerDesigns

Printed in Great Britain
by Amazon

79528267R00046